DIP IT!

70 Quick and Easy Recipes for Simply Delicious Dips

BARRY BLUESTEIN and KEVIN MORRISSEY

CB

CONTEMPORARY
BOOKS

CHICAGO

Library of Congress Cataloging-in-Publication Data

Bluestein, Barry.
    Dip it! : 70 quick and easy recipes for simply delicious dips /
Barry Bluestein and Kevin Morrissey.
      p.   cm.
    ISBN 0-8092-4175-7 : $7.95
    1. Dips (Appetizers)   I. Morrissey, Kevin.   II. Title.
TX740.B56   1990
641.8'12—dc20   89-48251
                                          CIP

Published by Contemporary Books, Inc.
180 North Michigan Avenue, Chicago, Illinois 60601
Manufactured in the United States of America
International Standard Book Number: 0-8092-4175-7

Published simultaneously in Canada by Beaverbooks, Ltd.
195 Allstate Parkway, Valleywood Business Park
Markham, Ontario L3R 4T8 Canada

Contents

With heartfelt dedication to Cecelia "Cis" Hartman,
who was always there with an answer and a loaf of bread.

Acknowledgments

We wish to gratefully acknowledge the support of Barbara Grunes, who has believed in us and in Season To Taste Books from the beginning. Barbara has been a mentor, a model, and a mensch whenever needed.

Heartfelt thanks to Claudia Clark Potter, Mary McLaughlin, Kathleen Rybak, and Elaine Barlas for their continual assistance, willing stomachs, hand holding, and clear vision of light at the bottom of the dip bowl. We also wish to thank all those who inspired dips or lent their culinary fetishes to our muse.

And we raise a chip to our editor, Linda Gray, who proves over and over again that mild-mannered editors for major metropolitan publishing houses still have shirtsleeves to roll up and pens faster than a speeding bullet.

1
Introduction

To put it simply, Americans love to dip. We have an enduring passion for the ritual of taking aim with a morsel of finger food and an addiction to the seemingly endless varieties of concoctions that lie at the end of the swing. Through several decades of radical changes in eating habits and far-flung food fads, from our first cadged samples of our parents' cocktail party dips right on down through fondue, guacamole, and hummus, we continue to sink our chips into this favorite of all finger foods.

Of course, dips have grown up quite a bit over the years. No longer just "a cup of sour cream and a package of onion soup mix," these days dips are likely to be found in the form of fresh tarragon, roasted peppers, oysters, artichokes, Gorgonzola cheese, and mangoes. Spicy Far Eastern dipping sauces, provocative curries, European delicacies, and silky dessert blends now share the dip table with the old classics.

We think dips are the ideal food for today's eclectic tastes and harried lifestyles. Far more than mere chip fodder, dips bring out the best in veggies, seafood, breads, meats, poultry, and fruit. They travel well to the picnic grove and to the beach. They can be served as appetizers, party fare, or light snacks, and they can be paired with a variety of dippers to make a full meal. Furthermore, dips can be made ahead of time, stored in the refrigerator, and brought to the table in minutes when unexpected company arrives or midnight munchies descend. They're also economical, with the cost of large (party-size) quantities of dips usually amounting to only a few cents per serving.

To help you make the most of your dipping, we've included a "diptionary" of information on the bases, ingredients, preparation, and presentation of dips. Each recipe has suggested dip and dipper pairings. You'll also find creative, easy-to-make dipper recipes, ranging from the basic potato chip to the trendy elephant garlic chip, along with tips on preparing just about every kind of vegetable and meat dipper imaginable.

So grab a spoon, pull out a mixing bowl, and enjoy! After all, as versatile, easy, and economical as dips are, you know what the real motivation is here. Dips are fun. Forget what your mother told you about not playing with your food, eating with your fingers, or snacking between meals. Dips are gooey, glorious, and eminently gratifying—the last guilt-free refuge in a world turned all too serious about food. Dip in!

2
Diptionary

BASES

Although dips come in countless varieties, most start with one of the following bases, to which seasonings and ingredients are added to give each dip its own distinctive flavor and personality. Each base has its own character and is particularly suited to bringing out the best in different types of ingredients. Likewise, the base will influence what kind of dipper is called for.

Sour Cream. The classic base of the good old-fashioned, all-American chip dip, sour cream is a perennial favorite because it mixes so well with a wide range of flavorings. Its smooth consistency and slightly tangy flavor make it a good companion for veggies of all sorts, and its stark whiteness simply begs for the addition of colorful specks. Sour cream dips should be thoroughly chilled before serving to allow the flavors of all the other ingredients to infuse into the sour cream.

People on low-fat diets can be consoled by the knowledge that yogurt can easily be substituted for sour cream in most cases.

Cream Cheese. Cream cheese added to sour cream is the royalty of dip bases as far as we're concerned. The two are perfect foils for each other's inherent tastes, resulting in a neutral base that allows the flavor of other ingredients to stand out. The addition of cream cheese to sour cream also thickens the mixture sufficiently so that heavier ingredients (such as diced vegetables) will float in the dip instead of sinking to the bottom of the bowl. (Note: don't try to use cream cheese alone as a base for dry ingredients. It will most likely do in even the sturdiest of dippers unless it's mixed with something more liquid.)

Buy cream cheese in block form. The whipped variety in the tub has air whipped into it, which will wreak havoc with your measurements. Before blending with other ingredients, let the cream cheese soften to room temperature and then "cream" it—mash it to a smooth consistency with a sturdy spoon in a mixing bowl (this is fairly easy to do by hand once the cheese has softened and can also be accomplished with the help of various appliances discussed later).

Mayonnaise. The traditional dressing of Europe, mayonnaise is now at home as a base for New World dips. Its natural blandness makes an ideal backdrop for herb flavorings, which it tends to absorb quickly. Mayonnaise is often successfully teamed with sour cream. Mayo-based dips are best with veggie and seafood dippers, as well as with any meat that you might use in a salad.

Mayo dips must be watched carefully and absolutely cannot be left out in the heat, as the raw egg yolks in mayonnaise give it a very short life span.

Although you certainly can use the convenient, store-bought kind, you might want to try our recipe for homemade mayonnaise—it tastes better and is relatively easy to make. We've written our mayonnaise-based dip recipes on the assumption that store-bought mayo will be the first choice of most folks. If using our homemade, omit any additional oil called for in these recipes.

Our Homemade Mayo

3 egg yolks
2½ teaspoons lemon juice
⅛ teaspoon white pepper
⅛ teaspoon salt
1¼ cups vegetable oil

Using a food processor: Fit a food processor with steel blade and place egg yolks, lemon juice, pepper, and salt in a bowl. Blend until smooth. While continuing to process, very slowly drizzle oil through the feed tube. Continue until all oil is used and mayonnaise thickens.

By hand: Using a whisk, beat egg yolks, lemon juice, pepper, and salt until blended. Slowly add oil by the ½ teaspoon, whisking constantly. Continue until all oil is used and mayonnaise is thickened.

Makes 1¾ cups

Yogurt and Cottage Cheese. Yogurt is often the costar of a dip base, used either to thin the mixture or to impart a tangier flavor. Be sure to use plain, unflavored yogurt (vanilla will *not* do).

We're rather partial to using cottage cheese, which adds an interesting texture to dips. A dip base that includes cottage cheese holds up to the addition of large chunks of vegetables and works particularly well with cracker dippers. In some recipes, cottage cheese must first be creamed, as you would cream cream cheese (in this case, you're breaking up the curds).

Beans. Bean dips came onto the scene with the widespread emergence of ethnic food some 20 years ago and have remained extremely popular ever since. Beans mix well with cheeses and strong spices, producing distinctive, earthy-colored dips that are best accompanied by chip and bread dippers. As most bean dips are ethnic in derivation, we recommend pairing them with dippers of similar origins (Middle Eastern garbanzo bean dip with pita triangles, for example).

Dried beans, which are less expensive than the canned variety, must first be soaked for several hours and then cooked until fork-tender. Canned beans are already cooked and thus more convenient but come packed in floured water that must be thoroughly rinsed off before you use them.

INGREDIENTS

Think of your base as a blank canvas on which you are now about to create a dipstronomical masterpiece. The next step is preparation of the various ingredients that will give life to your creation.

Herbs. The aroma of fresh herbs and the difference they can make in the appearance of your dip say much in their favor. With some herbs, such as basil, using the fresh variety will actually tint the base of the dip. We recommend using fresh herbs when the herb is the primary ingredient flavoring the dip and in dips where we feel the herb's fresh flavor is essential. Remember to chop herbs fine before adding them to the dip mixture.

Vegetables. Always use fresh veggies in your dip unless the recipe specifies otherwise. Most of our recipes call for raw vegetables, which add a lively crunch to the mixture. In the few dips where roasting or baking are part of the preparation, just follow our step-by-step directions.

Seafood. We recommend the use of canned seafood in dips. It's convenient and in the case of ingredients such as smoked oysters or sardines, the only form in which they are readily available. Always be sure to rinse seafood (fresh or canned) thoroughly in a strainer under cold running water before adding to the dip.

For *shrimp* dips, buy the tiniest baby shrimp you can find. If you use larger shrimp, dice them coarsely before combining with other ingredients.

When using *crabmeat*, flake with a fork after draining and pick out any filament that may remain.

Canned *tuna* should be purchased packed in water so as not to add excess oil to the dip. With canned seafood that usually comes packed in oil, such as *oysters* and *anchovies*, thoroughly drain off the oil. *Sardines* and *salmon*, even out of the can, may contain bits of skin and bone that must be carefully removed.

For *caviar* dips, buy the cheapest caviar available. This is not to deny the merits of fine caviar. But, trust us, the cheap stuff holds its flavor and its shape better when blended with other ingredients.

EQUIPMENT

Dips are not only fun, they're easy to make as well. In most cases, the only equipment you really need, other than a mixing bowl, a sturdy spoon, a chopping knife, and a strainer when draining and rinsing are called for, is a strong arm!

Nonetheless, we don't want to see all that high-tech gadgetry in your kitchen go to waste. It can be used to make the preparation of dips even faster and easier—thus conserving vital arm muscles for the end object of dipping.

In the art and science of dipstronomy, as in most culinary endeavors, the *food processor* once again proves itself to be just about the niftiest invention since potato chips. By following the manufacturer's directions for your particular model, you can use your food processor for finely dicing solid dip ingredients or chopping fresh herbs, pureeing vegetables or beans, creaming cottage cheese or cream cheese, and, with the proper disc, shredding block cheeses.

A *blender* can also be used to puree beans, chop herbs, cream cottage cheese and (with the addition of a little liquid from the recipe) cream cream cheese. An *electric mixer* can simplify the task of creaming cottage cheese or cream cheese.

CHILLING AND WARMING

Many of our dips call for chilling, to allow the flavors to be infused (if you try a mouthful right after mixing and then again after chilling, you'll be surprised at the difference). For these recipes, cover dips tightly and refrigerate for at least 2 hours. These dips can also be made up to 24 hours in advance and refrigerated. Garnish the dip after chilling.

When serving chilled dips, especially in the case of those with mayonnaise or sour cream bases, it is a good idea to place the dip bowl within a larger, shallower bowl filled with shaved ice. This will maintain optimal temperature, keep the dip from separating, and guard against spoilage.

Hot dips should be prepared on the stove top or in the oven according to individual recipe directions. For serving, transfer the dip to a chafing dish or fondue pot over a low warming flame. Be careful to use only heat-resistant utensils.

PRESENTATION

The way in which you present your dips can make a highly personal statement, rather like putting your signature on a finished work of art.

Dips are best served in glass or china bowls, which are free of the acidity found in metal bowls. Lining dip bowls with leaves of lettuce, radicchio, or endive adds a nice touch, as do colorful garnishes on top. Where we haven't suggested a particular garnish, reserve a tablespoon of one of the ingredients to place in a dollop in the center or sprinkle over the top. Depending upon the ingredients in the dip, you can also sprinkle peels of carrot or apple, shredded cabbage, chopped parsley, lemon zest, or shredded cheese over your masterpiece.

Dippers, especially vegetable dippers that lend themselves to fanciful arrangements, are often placed in a star-burst pattern or scattered on a platter in clusters. In either case, intersperse dippers of varying colors and textures.

STORING

Always store dips in the refrigerator. Use only glass, china, or plastic containers, as the acidity in metal bowls can alter the color and taste of the dip. Seal tightly (airtight containers are best) to prevent the dip from absorbing other refrigerator smells or turning crusty on the top. Stir before serving again.

3
The Big Dipper

Just as the right wine can make a meal, the ultimate success of a dip is dependent upon the dipper. Throughout this book, we've recommended pairings that we think will do your dips proud.

The possibilities are just about endless, limited only by your ingenuity and your taste buds. To help you get started, we've provided suggestions for homemade chip, cracker, and bread dippers, prepping instructions for vegetables and fruit to be used as dippers, and directions for preparing some of the more popular seafood, poultry, and meat dippers.

CHIPS

The age-old standard-bearers of dipping, chips are the frontline soldiers traditionally thrust forward by those armies of outstretched arms advancing upon the dip table.

While we feel it would be somewhat disrespectful to disparage the troops that have seen the most action (and hence we include homemade potato chips and tortilla chips), one need not be limited by tradition. Therefore, you'll also find recipes for preparing a number of novel variations, including elephant garlic chips, butterflake biscuit chips, noodle chips, and potato skins. You may also want to try toasted bagel chips. Just cut a bagel into slices as thin as possible and toast them until golden brown.

Easy-to-Make Homemade Potato Chips

Scrub 6 to 7 medium potatoes (about 2 pounds) under cold running water and peel if desired. Slice the potatoes as thinly as possible (thin enough to see through). As you proceed, place the slices in a bowl of cold water to remove starch. The water will turn white. Drain and refill the bowl, repeating this until the water remains clear. Drain and let the potatoes dry.

Fill a heavy skillet halfway with vegetable oil or melted vegetable shortening and cook over medium heat until oil crackles. Place potato slices into the hot oil a few at a time, taking care not to overcrowd the pan. When potatoes are brown on both sides (4 to 6 minutes), remove from pan and drain on paper towels. Sprinkle with salt if desired.

Makes approximately 180 chips, or enough for
about 3 cups of dip

Tortilla Chips

These dippers can be made from either flour or corn tortillas. Corn tortillas are the more familiar breed, from which the dippers served with salsa in Mexican restaurants are made. We cut them into either triangular chips or small strips. Fried flour tortillas, which we've found hold up better in the larger chip form, have a stronger, deep-fried taste, more like a tostada.

Cut tortilla into thin strips (12 to 16 per tortilla) or into triangles (8 per tortilla).

Fill a heavy skillet halfway with vegetable oil or melted vegetable shortening and cook over medium heat until oil crackles. Put tortilla strips or triangles into the hot oil a few at a time. Watch carefully, as they fry very quickly (in approximately 30 seconds). When brown on both sides, remove from pan and drain on paper towels.

10 whole tortillas make enough chips for about 1½ cups of dip

Edible Tortilla Baskets

A tortilla basket will lend flair to your dip table and set off a Mexican dip nicely. Fill a heavy skillet halfway with vegetable oil or melted vegetable shortening and cook over medium heat until oil crackles. Have ready an empty 1-pound coffee can (washed, free of grounds, and very thoroughly dried).

Place tortilla in hot oil, being careful of spattering. Protecting your hand with an oven mitt, grasp the coffee can with tongs, position it over center of the submerged tortilla, and lower onto tortilla. Continue to hold down until tortilla turns golden brown and begins to rise up around the coffee can, forming a tulip shape (about 2 to 3 minutes). Put coffee can aside. Remove tortilla basket and drain on paper towels. Let cool.

Elephant Garlic Chips

Peel 6 elephant garlic cloves and slice lengthwise as thinly as possible (about 12 slices per clove).

Fill a heavy skillet halfway with vegetable oil or melted vegetable shortening and cook over medium heat until oil crackles. Put garlic slices into hot oil a few at a time and watch closely. As soon as the outer edges begin to brown (approximately 15 seconds), turn the chips over. Fry each chip until the other side turns brown (not black—approximately 15 seconds). Be careful, as the second side cooks very quickly.

6 cloves make enough chips for about 1 cup of dip

Butterflake Biscuit Chips

Prepare refrigerated butterflake biscuit mix according to package directions and let biscuits cool thoroughly. (Leftover butterflake biscuits can be used or biscuits can be made the night before and stored in a zip-lock bag.)

Separate the flaky layers of each biscuit. Place on an ungreased cookie sheet and bake at 250° F for 25 to 30 minutes, or until crisp. Let sit for about 45 minutes before serving.

One package of biscuit mix makes 5 to 6 dozen chips, or enough for about 2 cups of dip

Noodle Chips

Boil wide egg noodles in water according to package directions. When cooked, strain immediately and run under cold water. Let noodles cool and dry on paper towels. Cut each noodle into 3-inch lengths.

Fill a heavy skillet halfway with vegetable oil or melted vegetable shortening and cook over medium heat until oil crackles. Put noodles into hot oil a few at a time and fry until golden (about 1 minute). Remove from pan and drain on paper towels.

One 8-ounce package of noodles makes approximately 120 chips, or enough for about 2 cups of dip

Potato Skins

Scrub 6 to 7 medium baking potatoes (about 2 pounds) under cold running water and dry. Bake at 400° F for 40 minutes. Remove and let cool. Cut each potato in half lengthwise and scoop out the meat, leaving about a quarter-inch of potato lining in each skin. Reserve the scooped out insides for making miniature potato pancakes (see recipe on page 15). Cut each hollowed-out potato skin into quarters (yielding 4 chips per skin, or 8 chips from each whole potato). Brush with melted butter on both sides. Bake at 425° F for 15 minutes, or until crisp.

6 potatoes make enough potato skins for about 2 cups of dip

CRACKERS

While there are numerous advantages to homemade chips, crackers are another story entirely. Crackers come packaged in just about any flavor, shape, or size you'll ever want; and the truth is that commercial preparation of crackers usually yields better results.

Recognizing, however, that there are those dedicated do-it-yourselfers among you whose shirtsleeves just will not stay rolled down, we offer a recipe for a tasty homemade onion cracker.

Onion Crackers

2 cups all-purpose flour
1 teaspoon baking soda
⅛ teaspoon salt
2 tablespoons vegetable shortening
½ cup minced onion
1½ teaspoons celery seed
¾ teaspoon crushed red pepper flakes
⅔ cup water (approximately)

In a food processor fitted with a metal blade, combine flour, baking soda, and salt and blend. Add shortening all at once and process until mixture becomes coarse meal. Add onion, celery seed, and red pepper flakes. Drizzle water through the feed tube a little at a time, using only as much water as necessary for batter to form a ball (amount of water will vary with every batch).

Divide dough in half. On a well-floured board, roll out each half at a time to ⅛-inch thickness. Cut into squares or rectangles with a knife or pizza cutter.

Place crackers on a lightly greased cookie sheet and pierce each three times with a fork. Bake at 350° F for 20 to 25 minutes, or until medium brown. Cool on a rack.

Makes 50 to 60 crackers, or enough for about 2 cups of dip

BREADS

To withstand the test of dipping, breads must be firm enough in texture and body to successfully transport the dip from bowl to mouth. Chunks of coarser breads, such as French, Italian, and some ryes, work well, as do toasted or dried breads. Pita bread cut into triangles and toasted is a tasty and versatile dipper. Our suggestions follow for quick herbed croutons and bread sticks.

Herbed Croutons

Using 4 cups of crustless bread that is fresh or one day old, cut into 2-inch squares or tear into chunks. (You can also use corn bread.) Gently toss bread chunks with 1 cup melted butter that has been laced with herbs (see variations below). Place on a cookie sheet and toast in a 400° F oven for 10 to 15 minutes if a soft center is desired or for 20 to 25 minutes for crunchier croutons.

Makes enough for about 2½ cups of dip

Variation 1: *2 tablespoons dried tarragon*
½ teaspoon onion powder
Variation 2: *2 cloves garlic, crushed in a garlic press*
¼ teaspoon salt
Variation 3: *1 clove garlic, crushed in a garlic press*
1 tablespoon dried basil
Grated Parmesan cheese for garnish (sprinkle over croutons just before toasting)
Variation 4: *2 tablespoons Italian seasoning*
Variation 5: *2 tablespoons minced onion*
¼ teaspoon salt

Bread Sticks

Melt ¼ cup butter and mix with ¼ teaspoon garlic powder. Prepare frozen soft bread sticks according to package directions, but brush with garlic butter before baking. When done, let cool for about 2 hours.

Cut each bread stick into 4 equal pieces. Place on ungreased cookie sheet and bake at 225° F for 30 minutes, or until bread sticks are dry and crisp.

One package of frozen bread sticks makes enough for about 2½ cups of dip

VEGETABLES

The crudité craze of the 1970s awakened Americans to the hidden potential of vegetables. No longer overcooked, soggy, and tasteless, vegetables are now enjoyed raw—crisp, flavorful, and in their most nutritious form—or lightly steamed, dipped in a variety of yummy accompaniments.

Firm varieties, such as carrot sticks, celery stalks, or flowerets of cauliflower and broccoli, will stand up to even the densest of dips. Some smaller veggies, such as cherry tomatoes or brussels sprouts, may require utensils (such as toothpicks or mini skewers) to spear the dipper, lest you risk its loss at sea in the dip bowl.

Always remember to wash vegetables first, dry them thoroughly, and chill. To chill, wrap veggies in damp paper towels, place in an unsealed plastic bag, and set in the refrigerator overnight. Following are the prepping instructions for some of our favorite veggie dippers.

Asparagus: Break off the tough, woody end at the base of each spear.

Artichoke: Cut stem flush with base and clip the sharp point at the tip of each leaf with scissors. Steam for 45 minutes, or until fork tender. After cooling, cut in half vertically and remove fuzzy choke (a grapefruit spoon works best). Serve halves cut side down so that leaves can be pulled off easily.

Bok Choy: Separate leaves, discarding any yellow or very dark green parts.

Broccoli: Cut off the stalk, remove leaves, and cut into flowerets.

Brussels Sprouts: Remove tough outer leaves and trim the bottoms, as you would for cooking. Let soak a few minutes in cold water to crisp. Serve whole or halved, depending upon size.

Carrots: Peel or scrub (remember that the greatest vitamin content is in the skin), trim ends, and cut in half horizontally; then cut vertically into thin strips. Carrots can also be cut horizontally into circles.

Cabbage: Remove outer leaves and stalk; cut into strips thick enough to hold together, retaining a piece of core on each wedge.

Cauliflower: Remove outer leaves and stalk and cut into flowerets.

Celery: Trim off leaves and cut into strips or wedges.

Celery Root: Trim top and cut the root, which is shaped something like a turnip, into strips or wedges, then peel.

Chicory or Belgian Endive: Not to be confused with the curly or leafy green variety. Has a slightly bitter flavor. Cut into thin strips or dipping size wedges.

Chili Peppers: Including jalapeño peppers. Cut in half lengthwise and carefully remove seeds. Rinse under cold water and cut into strips. Remember that this stuff has quite a kick—wear rubber gloves when prepping and be sure to forewarn your guests.

Corn: Serve individual ears of pickled baby corn. (It's OK to eat the cobs.)

Cucumber: Trim ends, peel if desired, cut in half horizontally and then into thin strips. Or cut cucumber horizontally into rounds.

Fennel: Trim off and discard wispy, fernlike leaves at top and ends. Cut into dipping size strips. Has a pleasant, aniselike flavor.

Green Onions or Scallions: Peel off outer layer, cut tip off root end, and trim green ends.

Jicama: Remove ends, peel, and slice thinly.

Mushrooms: Trim off stump end and wipe clean with a damp paper towel or a mushroom brush. Do not soak in water. Use whole or halved, depending upon size.

Peppers: Seed and slice green, red, yellow, or purple bell peppers into strips. Can also be cut into wider, scooplike wedges. The combination of two or three of the varieties makes an attractive mix.

Radishes: Trim off root and stem ends. Sculpt to your heart's content if you're so inclined, after soaking radishes in ice water to crisp for a couple of hours.

Snow Peas: Simply trim off both ends and remove strings.

Squash: Yellow or green varieties of zucchini. Trim off top and bottom and cut into dipping size strips, circles, or wedges.

String Beans: Use either green beans or wax beans, or both, to add color. Snap off ends of beans and remove string.

Tomatoes: Use whole cherry tomatoes or wedges of plum or round tomatoes.

Turnips: Cut off the top and root ends of a young turnip, peel or scrub, and cut into thin slices (like a carrot).

Miniature Potato Pancakes

Rather at the opposite end of the spectrum from crisp, raw veggies lies another of our favorite dippers, one that at least began life in the vegetable kingdom—miniature potato pancakes. They're delicious and practical, since they can be made weeks in advance and reheated.

2 cups diced raw potato
2 eggs, beaten
1½ teaspoons salt
Black pepper to taste
1 tablespoon grated yellow onion
¼ cup vegetable oil

Place potato in strainer and run under cold water to remove starch. Shake well. Place in a food processor or blender and chop fine. Add egg, salt, pepper, and onion and mix well. In a 10-inch skillet, heat vegetable oil until it crackles. Drop batter by tablespoonful into hot oil and fry until golden brown (about 5 minutes per side). Drain on paper towels.

Once cooled, pancakes may be frozen. Place in a freezer-safe container, making sure they don't overlap and put a double thickness of wax paper between each layer. Reheat on cookie sheet at 350° F until hot and crisp.

*Makes approximately 50 pancakes, or enough for about
2 cups of dip*

FRUIT

Foolish consistency is the hobgoblin of a small dip table, as they say, and man does not live by chips alone. To experience the full spectrum of dipping, one must savor the particular pleasure of scooping a mouthful of cheesecake dip on a slice of melon or plunging a strawberry into chocolate dipping sauce.

As with veggies, you can let your imagination run amok, using the following suggestions merely as points of departure. Here, too, always wash fruit carefully, dry, and chill. Use firm fruit. Some, as we indicate below, should be dunked in an acid bath, which will keep the fruit from turning brown. To make the acid bath, just add 2 teaspoons of lemon juice to 2 cups of water. After dunking fruit in bath, drain on paper towels.

Apples: Peel if desired, core, and cut into wedges. Requires acid bath.
Apricots: Remove pits and quarter. Requires acid bath.

Bananas: Use firm bananas, free of bruises. Just peel and cut on the diagonal into wedges. Requires acid bath.

Coconuts: Remove outer shell, reserve milk for other uses if desired, and cut coconut meat into dipping size strips or chunks. Rinse with cold water.

Figs: Remove stem end and quarter.

Grapefruit: Remove peel, then break into segments. Carefully remove seeds and white pith.

Guava: Remove skin. Cut into wedges and carefully remove seeds.

Kiwis: Remove skin from firm kiwis and quarter or cut into circles.

Mangoes: Remove skin. Cut top half of fruit away from large oval pit. Turn over, cut away balance of fruit, and discard pit. Cut fruit into wedges across the grain.

Melons: Cantaloupe, crenshaw, and casaba melons, like most fruit, complement sweeter dips, while honeydews are a good accompaniment to saltier or spicier dips. In any case, cut off outer skin, cut in half, scoop out seeds, and cut pulp into dipping size slices, chunks, or wedges.

Nectarines: Pit and quarter. Requires acid bath.

Oranges: Peel and separate into individual segments. Carefully remove seeds.

Papayas: Use ripe papaya. Remove rind, cut in half, and scoop out seeds. Cut into thin strips.

Peaches: Remove pit and cut into wedges. Requires acid bath.

Pearapples: Remove core and cut into slices or wedges. Requires acid bath.

Pears: Peel if desired, core, and cut into dipping size chunks. Requires acid bath.

Pineapples: Remove outer skin, cut out the eyes, and remove center core if desired. Cut into chunks or spears.

Plums: Cut in half, pit, and quarter firm plums.

Prickly Pears or Cactus Pears: Using a fork to hold fruit in place, remove rind. Cut into slices or wedges.

Star Fruit or Carambola: White or sweet yellow varieties. Cut fruit horizontally into stars.

Strawberries: Serve whole.

Tangerines: Peel and separate into individual segments. Carefully remove seeds.

Dried fruits not to be overlooked include apples, apricots, banana chips, pitted dates, figs, pears, and pineapples.

SEAFOOD

What we're primarily talking about here is shrimp, the hands-down, all-time favorite of most cocktail party aficionados. Salmon may be known for joining forces in their journey upstream, but no one has truly witnessed a school of fish in action until they've seen a bevy of shrimp dippers converging with full force on the remoulade. In addition to shrimp, we include suggestions on serving up a few other creatures from the deep.

Shrimp: Shell, score down the back (making an incision about $1/16$ inch deep), and remove the thin black vein while holding under cold running water. Bring a pot of water to a boil (about 2 quarts of water for a pound of large shrimp). Add a little salt, throw in the shrimp, turn off the flame, and let stand for about 5 minutes, until shrimp just curl and turn pink and translucent. Do not overcook! Then drain, run the shrimp under cold water, and refrigerate.

Crab Claws: Stone crab claws are readily available already cooked. Just smash the shells with a nutcracker and place in a bowl over ice.

Crab Legs: King crab legs and snow crab legs also are readily available cooked. Break into lengths at the joints and crack shells with a nutcracker.

Crayfish: Follow directions for preparing shrimp.

Lobster: Use large lobster tails. Bring a pot of water to a boil (about 2 quarts of water for a pound of lobster). Plunge tails in boiling water and return to a boil. When shell turns orange, lower to simmer and cook until meat at the end of the tail turns translucent. Remove and blanch under cold water. Split the soft underside of the shell with scissors, remove meat, and cut into chunks.

Sarimi: Imitation crab. Sold cooked and chunked in most supermarkets.

Fresh Oysters: Loosen the oyster from the bottom shell and serve on the half shell over a bed of ice (allowing guest to scoop up dip with oyster on the shell).

Smoked Oysters: Drain and serve each with a toothpick.

MEAT AND POULTRY

As long as you've eaten your vegetable dippers, you can proceed to the rest of the goodies on the dip table. Meat and poultry dippers will win the hearts and minds of those guests who anticipated leaving your party having had only a handful of potato chips to stave off starvation.

Chicken Breasts: Poach breasts in wine and cube for serving. Or marinate breasts in teriyaki sauce, bake, and cube for serving.

Chicken Drumettes: The drumsticklike part of the leg. Marinate if desired, then fry.

Chicken Satay: Skewer cooked, sliced chicken breast on a wooden stick for dipping.

Deli Meat: Cut rolls of cooked, sliced roast beef, ham, corned beef, or pastrami into 3- to 4-inch lengths.

Duck: Cut cooked or smoked breast into strips.

Ham: Cut cooked, smoked, maple-cured, or honey-cured ham into thin 3-inch strips or into 1-inch cubes.

Hot Dogs: Serve miniature cooked hot dogs whole, or cut cooked regular-size hot dogs into slices on the diagonal.

Precooked Sausages: Use bologna, summer sausage, any variety of salami, or other cooked sausage cut into ½-inch lengths, then wedged.

Raw Sausages: Try pork, beef, veal, duck, or Polish. Prick skin, broil until brown, and cut into 2-inch lengths.

Steak: Marinate tenderloin or sirloin in teriyaki sauce, broil, and cube.

Turkey: Cut cooked or smoked breast into strips or cubes.

Beef Satay

One of the more popular dippers to surface of late is beef satay, or beef on a stick. It's easy to eat and filling, and meat as a dipper is still something of a novelty.

> **1 1-pound sirloin tip steak**
> **½ cup bottled teriyaki sauce**
> **2 teaspoons finely chopped green onion (white part only)**
> **Wooden or bamboo skewers**

Thinly slice steak. Slices should be about ½ inch shorter than the skewers on which they will be placed. Put meat, sauce, and green onion in a zip-lock bag, mix thoroughly, squeeze excess air from bag, and seal. Marinate at room temperature for 1 hour or in refrigerator for at least 3 hours. (Steak can be marinated overnight for a stronger taste.)

Soak skewers in water for 10 minutes before using. Weave skewer in and out through slice of beef, leaving a ½-inch "handle" at the bottom. Repeat until all slices are skewered. Broil about 2½ minutes, or to preferred doneness.

4
A Fine Kettle of Fish
SEAFOOD DIPS

LOWER EAST SIDE LOX

RED SOCKEYE SALMON SPECIAL

BABY SHRIMP AND TARRAGON MUSTARD

CAVIAR, DILL, AND PURPLE ONION

CIS'S CREAMED HERRING

CONTEMPLATING CAPE COD CLAM

SAUCY SARDINE

COCKTAIL CRAB

CAESAR MAYO

DRUNKEN TUNA

Lower East Side Lox

You don't have to be on Orchard Street to get into the spirit of this deli delight. Just "schmear" some on a bagel chip and enjoy.

1 cup cream cheese, softened
½ cup sour cream
½ cup lox or smoked salmon, cubed
¼ cup chopped fresh chives *or* 4 teaspoons dried
2 tablespoons chopped white onion
⅛ teaspoon white pepper
1 teaspoon whipping cream

Beat cream cheese to a smooth consistency and blend in sour cream. Mix in lox thoroughly. Stir in all other ingredients. Cover and chill.

Makes about 2½ cups

Suggested dippers: *bagel chips, tomatoes, radishes, cucumber, scallions, figs*

Red Sockeye Salmon Special

When late-night hunger pangs set in, we recommend that you fly straight to this hearty dip.

    ¾ **cup salmon (fresh or 1 7.5-ounce can, well drained),**
       flaked
    1 tablespoon lemon juice
    ½ **teaspoon finely diced white onion**
    1½ **teaspoons chopped fresh dill** *or* ½ **teaspoon dried**
    ½ **cup mayonnaise**
    ¼ **cup whipping cream**

Remove any remaining skin and bones from salmon (even canned salmon may have some). Mix with lemon juice, onion, and dill. Blend in mayonnaise and whipping cream. Cover and chill.

Makes about 1½ cups

Suggested dippers: *broccoli, cauliflower, cucumber, black bread, potato skins*

Baby Shrimp and Tarragon Mustard

A subtle yet pervasive hint of tarragon lends distinction to this version of the classic shrimp dip. Baby shrimp can be used whole; if using larger shrimp, coarsely dice.

> 2 tablespoons Dijon mustard
> 1 teaspoon lemon juice
> 1½ teaspoons white wine vinegar
> 2 tablespoons chopped fresh tarragon *or* 2 teaspoons
>   dried
> 1 cup mayonnaise
> ¾ cup baby shrimp
> ½ cup sour cream

Mix mustard, lemon juice, vinegar, and tarragon. Blend in mayonnaise. Add shrimp, then sour cream. Mix together well. Cover and chill.

Makes about 2½ cups

Suggested dippers: *butterflake biscuit chips, cabbage, chili peppers, string beans, artichoke leaves*

Caviar, Dill, and Purple Onion

While any caviar may be used in this dip, the full-bodied, supermarket black variety actually stands up to the other ingredients better than finer-grade caviar.

½ cup cream cheese, softened
¾ cup sour cream
1 3-ounce jar caviar
1 teaspoon lemon juice
1 tablespoon chopped fresh dill *or* 1 teaspoon dried
2 teaspoons diced purple onion
Chopped hard-boiled egg for garnish

Beat cream cheese to a smooth consistency. Blend in sour cream. Add remaining ingredients and mix well. Cover and chill. Garnish with chopped egg.

Makes about 1½ cups

Suggested dippers: *cocktail rye bread, toast triangles, cucumber, turnips, red bell pepper*

Cis's Creamed Herring

This Scandinavian delight comes from Cis, who is not Scandinavian, but who is a delight and has offered helpful advice on many a recipe.

> **1 4-ounce jar pickled herring in sour cream**
> **½ cup finely diced tart apple**
> **1 tablespoon finely diced white onion**
> **1 cup sour cream**

Puree herring (sauce and all) in a food processor or blender until smooth. Add all other ingredients and continue to process until smooth. Cover and chill.

Makes about 2 cups

Suggested dippers: *cocktail rye bread, lavasch crackers, broccoli, cherry tomatoes, zucchini*

Contemplating Cape Cod Clam

On a sultry August day when everyone you know seems to be off to Nantucket or Martha's Vineyard and you're stuck in the city with a broken air conditioner, the options are limited. If running away from home strikes you as a less than mature solution, make a pitcher of Cape Codders and take solace in this dip.

> ½ cup minced clams (fresh or 1 6½-ounce can, well
>   drained)
> 2 tablespoons clam juice
> 1 cup cream cheese, softened
> 1 tablespoon chili sauce
> ⅛ teaspoon hot sauce
> 1 tablespoon onion juice
> 1 teaspoon lemon juice
> ¼ teaspoon Worcestershire sauce

Blend clams, clam juice, and cream cheese to a smooth consistency. Add all other ingredients and mix well. Cover and chill.

Makes about 1¾ cups

Suggested dippers: *carrots, fennel, zucchini, wheat crackers*

Saucy Sardine

Devotees of the little devils will not be disappointed, as the other ingredients serve only to highlight this dip's robust sardine taste.

> **8 sardine fillets, skinned and boned**
> **1 cup sour cream**
> **2 tablespoons mayonnaise**
> **1 tablespoon chopped green onion (white and green parts)**
> **1 tablespoon chopped fresh parsley**
> **¼ teaspoon lemon juice**

Mash sardines with a fork. Blend in sour cream and mayonnaise. Add other ingredients and mix well. Cover and chill.

Makes about 1½ cups

Suggested dippers: *broccoli, cabbage, cherry tomatoes, carrots, pita triangles, cocktail rye bread, water crackers*

Cocktail Crab

The old adage "if you want something done right, do it yourself" comes into play here. While prepared cocktail sauce could be substituted for the first three ingredients, we have found that this recipe is far better tasting, and almost as easy to make from scratch.

> ¾ **cup catsup**
> 2 **tablespoons prepared horseradish**
> ⅛ **teaspoon hot sauce**
> ½ **cup crabmeat (fresh or 1 6-ounce can, well drained),**
>   **flaked**
> 1 **cup cream cheese, softened**
> 3 **tablespoons diced white onion**
> ⅛ **teaspoon salt**

Combine catsup, horseradish, and hot sauce. Remove any remaining filament from crabmeat. Add crabmeat to catsup mixture and continue to blend. Add all other ingredients and mix until smooth. Serve at room temperature.

Makes about 2½ cups

Suggested dippers: *salty potato chips, potato skins, green bell pepper, turnips*

Caesar Mayo

Fit for an emperor, this dip is a variation on the traditional salad dressing without egg—and, of course, without the salad. It can also do double duty as a flavorful sandwich spread.

2 anchovy fillets
1½ cups mayonnaise
1 teaspoon Dijon mustard
2 tablespoons Parmesan cheese
1 teaspoon Worcestershire sauce
1 tablespoon lemon juice
¼ teaspoon black pepper

Chop and mash anchovy fillets on a cutting board. Put in a bowl and blend in mayonnaise. Add remaining ingredients and mix well. Cover and chill.

Makes about 1¾ cups

Suggested dippers: *seafood, deli roast beef or turkey, radishes, broccoli, cauliflower, snow peas*

Drunken Tuna

A generous dash of brandy perks up the traditional tuna dip. After a few laps in this bowl, the fish might start swimming backwards.

> 1½ tablespoons brandy
> 1 cup cream cheese, softened
> ¼ cup sour cream
> ¼ cup mayonnaise
> ¾ cup tuna (fresh or 1 6½-ounce can, well drained), flaked
> 2 tablespoons minced green onion (white and green parts)
> 1 tablespoon lemon juice
> ⅛ teaspoon hot sauce
> ⅛ teaspoon salt

Beat brandy and cream cheese to a smooth and creamy consistency. Blend in sour cream and mayonnaise. Mix in tuna and green onion. Add remaining ingredients and mix thoroughly. May be served at room temperature or chilled.

Makes about 2½ cups

Suggested dippers: *onion crackers, French bread cubes, cheese crackers, celery root, cucumber, radishes, Monterey Jack cheese*

5
The Spice Rack
SPICED AND HERBED DIPS

OPEN SESAME–GINGER

CURRIED GARLIC

CAYENNE MAYONNAISE

BYE-BYE BIRDY CURRY

FENNEL SEED–ONION

TARRAGON-MUSTARD

COUNTRY CLUB SOUR CREAM AND DILL

CREAMY PURPLE ONION AND BASIL

HOTTER THAN HECK HORSERADISH

CLAUDIA'S CURRY-LIME

LEMON-TARRAGON

Open Sesame-Ginger

A distinctive blend, redolent of sesame and evocative of Arabian nights. Aladdin would approve.

> **3 tablespoons Dijon mustard**
> **½ teaspoon ground ginger**
> **2 teaspoons soy sauce**
> **1 teaspoon sesame oil**
> **½ teaspoon sesame seeds**
> **¼ teaspoon black pepper**
> **3 tablespoons chopped green onion (white and green parts)**
> **1 cup sour cream**

Mix mustard, ginger, and soy sauce, blending well. Blend in sesame oil. Add sesame seeds, pepper, and green onion and mix thoroughly. Blend in sour cream. Cover and chill.

Makes about 1¼ cups

Suggested dippers: *chicken strips or cubes, fried wonton, noodle chips, bok choy*

Curried Garlic

Blending these forceful yet complementary spices brings out the best in both.

> 1 cup plain yogurt
> 1 cup sour cream
> 1 teaspoon dry mustard
> 2 teaspoons curry powder
> 2 teaspoons garlic powder

Add each ingredient in order listed, blending constantly until all are well mixed. Cover and chill.

Makes about 2 cups

Suggested dippers: *zucchini, mushrooms, cherry tomatoes, deli meat, chicken drumettes*

Cayenne Mayonnaise

This simple, elegant, and intensely peppery mixture is a great companion for seafood dippers.

       1½ cups mayonnaise
       ½ cup sour cream
       ½-1 teaspoon cayenne pepper (to taste)

Mix all ingredients together well. Cover and chill.

Makes about 2 cups

Suggested dippers: *seafood chunks, pineapple, cherry tomatoes, rye or cheese crackers*

Bye-Bye Birdy Curry

This curry began its life married to a chicken. We liked it so well, we decided to scrap the chicken and convert the curry into a dip. The crushed pineapple subtly enhances the flavor.

2 cups water
1½ teaspoons lemon juice
1 Granny Smith apple, peeled
1 cup mayonnaise
1 cup finely diced celery
¾ cup crushed fresh pineapple (or 1 8¼-ounce can crushed pineapple, drained well)
2 teaspoons curry powder
½ teaspoon salt
¼ teaspoon black pepper
½ cup chopped cashews
¼ cup crumbled Gorgonzola or other blue-veined cheese

Mix water and lemon juice in a bowl. Slice apple and put slices into lemon water to soak. Set aside. Put mayonnaise in a serving bowl. Add celery, pineapple, curry powder, salt, and pepper and mix well. Fold in cashews. Remove apples from lemon water and dice. Stir into mixture. Mix in Gorgonzola. Cover and chill.

Makes about 2 cups

Suggested dippers: *pita triangles, bread chunks, radishes, scallions, turnips, bell peppers*

Fennel Seed-Onion

The subtle licoricelike flavor and aroma of fennel gives this dip its unique character, which is highlighted by the crunch of the seeds.

½ teaspoon fennel seeds
1 cup cream cheese, softened
1 cup sour cream
¼ cup minced white onion
½ teaspoon salt
¼ teaspoon black pepper
1 teaspoon paprika

Beat fennel seeds and cream cheese together until smooth. Whip in sour cream. Blend in other ingredients and mix well. Cover and chill.

Makes about 2 cups

Suggested dippers: *carrots, zucchini, turnips, crab, butterflake biscuit chips*

Tarragon-Mustard

A native of France, tarragon is one of the more aromatic members of the herb family. It's the star of this dip—and we highly recommend using fresh tarragon for the greatest impact. If you close your eyes and inhale as you ingest a mouthful, you can almost picture the French countryside.

**1 tablespoon chopped fresh tarragon *or* 1 teaspoon
   dried**
1 tablespoon white wine vinegar
1 tablespoon Dijon mustard
¼ teaspoon salt
¼ teaspoon black pepper
1 cup mayonnaise
½ cup sour cream

Mix tarragon and vinegar. Mix in mustard well, then add salt and pepper. Blend in mayonnaise, then sour cream. Cover and chill.

Makes about 1½ cups

Suggested dippers: *chicken strips or cubes, shrimp, asparagus, onion crackers*

Country Club Sour Cream and Dill

A "comfort dip" reminiscent of the sour cream and dill salad dressings served in club dining rooms from Maine to California. Best made with fresh dill because of its wonderful aroma.

3 tablespoons chopped fresh dill *or* 1 tablespoon dried
1 tablespoon lemon juice
1 cup sour cream
1 teaspoon salt
½ teaspoon white pepper
2 tablespoons grated white onion
1 cup mayonnaise

Mix dill and lemon juice to soften dill. Blend in other ingredients. Cover and chill.

Makes about 2¼ cups

Suggested dippers: *red cabbage, broccoli, zucchini, tomatoes, string beans, cocktail rye bread, seafood, apple, nectarine*

Creamy Purple Onion and Basil

This rich dip has a subtle bite and a distinctive, lingering flavor. Although dried basil can be substituted, fresh basil produces an appealing mint-green hue. Flecked with purple onion and carrot, it looks as good as it tastes.

1 cup cream cheese, softened
¼ cup chopped fresh basil *or* 4 teaspoons dried
1 cup sour cream
¼ cup shredded carrot
¼ cup chopped purple onion
¼ teaspoon salt
¼ teaspoon black pepper

Beat cream cheese to a smooth consistency, gradually adding basil. Blend in sour cream. Add remaining ingredients and mix well. Cover and chill.

Makes about 2½ cups

Suggested dippers: *unsalted potato chips, water crackers, green bell pepper, mushrooms, brussels sprouts, fennel, smoked deli meat*

Hotter Than Heck Horseradish

A pungent, versatile dip that makes a statement—loud and clear!

4 tablespoons prepared horseradish
1 teaspoon garlic powder
2 cups sour cream
1 teaspoon white pepper

Mix horseradish and garlic powder thoroughly. Add sour cream and white pepper, blending well. Cover and chill.

Makes about 2¼ cups

Suggested dippers: *rolls of sliced roast beef, steamed cauliflower, bell peppers, potato chips, snow peas*

Claudia's Curry-Lime

Our friend Claudia usually serves this dip with pitchers of margaritas on the patio. Both the dip and the margaritas have a soothing lime undertaste, and both, like Claudia, pack a surprising punch.

4 tablespoons lime juice
2 tablespoons Dijon mustard
1 teaspoon minced garlic
1 cup mayonnaise
Cayenne pepper to taste
1 tablespoon curry powder

Mix lime juice and mustard well. Add garlic. Whisk in mayonnaise. Mix in spices. Cover and chill.

Makes about 1½ cups

Suggested dippers: *chicken drumettes, onion crackers, chicory, cauliflower*

Lemon-Tarragon

If you take one part hollandaise recipe, one part bernaise recipe, and add a Mediterranean accent in the form of capers, you come up with this refreshing hybrid.

4 tablespoons chopped fresh tarragon *or*
   4 teaspoons dried
1 teaspoon lemon juice
1 cup mayonnaise
2 teaspoons capers

Mix all ingredients well. Cover and chill.

Makes about 1¼ cups

Suggested dippers: *seafood, turkey, French bread, fennel, yellow zucchini, carrots*

6
The Salad Bowl
VEGETABLE DIPS

CHILI CON CARROT

ROASTED RED AND GREEN PEPPER

QUICK BACON-SPINACH

OLIVE TAPENADE

CLASSY MUSTARD-GARLIC MAYO

TOM'S SPLENDIFEROUS GUACAMOLE

CREAMY AVOCADO WITH BACON

AZTEC PYRAMID AVOCADO

CIS'S NEIGHBOR'S CUCUMBER-DILL

EGGPLANT CAVIAR

NOT MISS LILY'S OLIVES

MARY'S GARLIC-MAYO

RANDY RED SALSA

GREEN CHILI SALSA

Chili Con Carrot

No "carne" in sight, but fresh carrots provide crunch and verve in this chili-spiked mixture.

½ **cup diced carrot**
2 **cups sour cream**
½ **cup diced yellow onion**
1 **tablespoon Dijon mustard**
1 **tablespoon chili powder**
1 **teaspoon ground cumin**
2 **tablespoons chopped fresh parsley** *or* 2 **teaspoons dried**

Combine all ingredients and mix thoroughly. Cover and chill.

Makes about 3 cups

Suggested dippers: *brussels sprouts, salami, cocktail rye bread*

Roasted Red and Green Pepper

The subtle, smoky flavor of roasted peppers pervades this dip. Specked with festive bits of red and green, it's perfect for Christmas party fare.

1 red bell pepper
1 green bell pepper
1½ cups mayonnaise
½ cup sour cream
2 tablespoons lemon juice
1 tablespoon chopped fresh parsley *or* 1 teaspoon
    dried
Additional parsley and paprika for garnish

Slice peppers in half vertically and remove seeds. Char under broiler on both sides (about 5 minutes per side). Remove and cool. Peel and dice peppers and set aside. Blend mayonnaise and sour cream until smooth. Mix in lemon juice and parsley. Mix in peppers. Cover and chill. Garnish with parsley and sprinkle with paprika.

Makes about 3 cups

Suggested dippers: *deli meat, elephant garlic chips, baby corn, string beans, carrots, bread sticks*

Quick Bacon-Spinach

Shortcuts are encouraged in preparing this thick, rich dip. We call for frozen chopped spinach, which works as well as fresh and saves you from having to do your own steaming and chopping. Bottled imitation bacon bits can be substituted for real bacon as well.

> 1 10-ounce package frozen chopped spinach, thawed
>   and drained
> ½ cup finely crumbled bacon (about 7 slices cooked)
>   *or* imitation bacon bits
> 1 cup mayonnaise
> 2¼ teaspoons chopped fresh dill *or* ¾ teaspoon dried
> ½ teaspoon garlic powder
> ⅛ teaspoon cayenne pepper

Squeeze as much water as possible from the spinach. Mix bacon and spinach. Add other ingredients and mix together well. Cover and chill.

Makes about 2¾ cups

Suggested dippers: *apple, fennel, zucchini, Monterey Jack or cheddar cheese, toast triangles, pear*

Olive Tapenade

Mayonnaise replaces oil in our rendition of the classic French tapenade, but the anchovies and olives remain to impart their salty, sassy magic.

2 anchovy fillets
1 cup chopped black olives
4 teaspoons Worcestershire sauce
½ cup mayonnaise
¼ cup chopped fresh parsley *or* 4 teaspoons dried
½ teaspoon salt
1 tablespoon minced garlic
3 tablespoons chopped fresh basil *or* 1 tablespoon dried

Chop and mash anchovies on a cutting board. Put in a bowl and mix with olives and Worcestershire sauce. Blend in mayonnaise. Add all other ingredients and mix well. Cover and chill.

Makes about 2 cups

Suggested dippers: *scallions, French bread, seafood*

Classy Mustard-Garlic Mayo

This quick and easy treat is a modern rendition of the classic Parisian remoulade.

> **1 tablespoon Dijon mustard**
> **½ teaspoon garlic powder**
> **1 cup mayonnaise**
> **1 tablespoon capers**
> **1 tablespoon chopped fresh tarragon *or* 1 teaspoon
>   dried**
> **1 tablespoon chopped fresh parsley *or* 1 teaspoon
>   dried**

Mix all ingredients well. Cover and chill.

Makes about 1¼ cups

Suggested dippers: *shrimp, crabmeat, duck, brussels sprouts, jicama, radishes*

Tom's Splendiferous Guacamole

Guacamole may have become a "cliché," but it's still just about everybody's favorite. Tom is beginning to hate the stuff, because no matter what other goodies he prepares, everyone always gushes about the guacamole. Jalapeño peppers and cilantro give this version an added kick, while the heavy dose of lime juice will keep it from discoloring during its probably brief stay on your dip table.

> **4 medium-large, very ripe avocados**
> **¼ cup lime juice**
> **2 cups diced fresh, ripe tomatoes**
> **1 cup diced yellow onion**
> **1 tablespoon diced jalapeño peppers**
> **¼ teaspoon hot sauce**
> **¼ cup finely chopped fresh cilantro *or* 4 teaspoons dried**
> **Additional cilantro and sour cream for garnish**

Peel and pit avocados, then coarsely mash in a bowl with a fork. Mix well with lime juice. Add other ingredients one at a time in order given, mixing thoroughly after each addition. Garnish with sour cream and sprinkle some cilantro on top. May be served at room temperature or chilled.

Makes about 5¼ cups

Suggested dippers: *warm tortilla chips, baby corn, black olives, jicama, mushrooms*

Creamy Avocado with Bacon

Creamy, tart, and very rich, this dip has a personality very distinct from its southern cousin, guacamole. The cucumber supplies a little crunch and is an interesting contrast to the avocado and bacon.

> **1 ripe avocado**
> **1 teaspoon lemon juice**
> **½ cup sour cream**
> **2 tablespoons finely crumbled bacon (1½-2 strips
>   cooked)** *or* **imitation bacon bits**
> **¼ teaspoon onion powder**
> **¼ teaspoon hot sauce**
> **2 tablespoons finely diced cucumber**

Peel, pit, and mash avocado with a fork. Mix with lemon juice. Blend in sour cream. Mix in other ingredients well. Cover and chill.

Makes about 1¼ cups

Suggested dippers: *green bell pepper, bok choy, celery, pita bread, radishes, aged cheddar cheese, cheese crackers*

Aztec Pyramid Avocado

This multilayered dip takes its inspiration from the famed Mexican ruins. In its simplest form it can be layered in a serving bowl. For more dramatic presentation, construct on a platter as a pyramid, with each layer smaller than the one below.

**3 California avocados (dark-skinned type), peeled and
   pitted
2 tablespoons lemon juice
1 cup cream cheese, softened
2 cups sour cream
1 package taco seasoning mix ($1\frac{5}{16}$ ounces)
2 cups shredded sharp cheddar cheese
3 cups finely chopped fresh tomatoes
5 green onions, sliced (white and light green parts)
$\frac{1}{2}$ cup sliced black olives**

Layer 1 (bottom): Mash avocados, mix well with lemon juice, and spread evenly in a bowl or on a serving plate to the edges of the dish.

Layer 2: Beat cream cheese to a smooth and creamy consistency. Blend in sour cream and mix in taco seasoning well. Spread over avocado layer.

Layer 3: Sprinkle cheddar cheese over cream cheese layer.

Layer 4: Distribute tomatoes over the cheddar cheese.

Layer 5: Spread green onions over the tomatoes.

Layer 6: Top with black olives.

Serve at room temperature.

Makes about 10½ cups

Suggested dippers: *tortilla chips, bell peppers, lobster, jicama*

Cis's Neighbor's Cucumber-Dill

Cool as a cucumber, this mixture came to us by way of our friend Cis's neighbor, a Turkish lady who remembers it from her homeland. We like to serve it alongside highly seasoned dips to help put out the fire.

> **1 medium cucumber**
> **¼ teaspoon white pepper**
> **2 tablespoons chopped fresh dill *or* 2 teaspoons dried**
> **1½ cups mayonnaise**
> **¾ cup sour cream**
> **¼ cup diced green bell pepper**

Skin, seed, and finely dice cucumber. Using a colander, squeeze out any excess water from cucumber chunks. Place in a bowl and mix well with pepper and dill. Blend in remaining ingredients and mix thoroughly. Cover and chill.

Makes about 3 cups

Suggested dippers: *broccoli, cauliflower, radishes, carrots, onion crackers*

Eggplant Caviar

This caviar comes not from sturgeon but from eggplant. We think it rivals the delicacy whose name it borrows.

1 medium eggplant (about 1 pound)
2 cloves garlic
½ teaspoon soy sauce
2 tablespoons olive oil
1 tablespoon lemon juice
1 cup chopped fresh tomato
2 tablespoons diced green onion (white and green parts)
2 tablespoons minced fresh parsley
1 tablespoon chopped fresh basil *or* 1 teaspoon dried

Cut eggplant in half lengthwise. Bake, cut side down, on a greased cookie sheet at 400° F for 60 minutes. As the eggplant cools, gently squeeze out excess water. Use a spoon to scoop pulp from the skin. Place pulp in a bowl and mash with a fork. Using a garlic press, crush garlic into eggplant. Add all other ingredients and mix well. Cover and chill.

Makes about 3½ cups

Suggested dippers: *sesame crackers, lavasch crackers, cocktail rye bread, scallions, bell peppers*

Not Miss Lily's Olives

Miss Lily serves up some of the best hors d'oeuvres in Greenwich Village, including meticulously stuffed olives. We like the concept of the olives but thought a recipe for putting the olives in the appetizer, instead of the other way around, would make the application easier.

> 1 cup cream cheese, softened
> 1 cup sour cream
> ¼ cup chopped black olives
> 2 tablespoons Worcestershire sauce
> 1 tablespoon paprika
> ½ teaspoon garlic powder
> 1 tablespoon chopped fresh parsley *or* 1 teaspoon
>   dried

Beat cream cheese to a smooth consistency. Blend in sour cream. Mix in all remaining ingredients. Cover and chill.

Makes about 2¼ cups

Suggested dippers: *scallions, jalapeño peppers, celery root, potato chips, duck sausage*

Mary's Garlic-Mayo

This mixture has a pungent garlic flavor that lingers on the taste buds. It goes well with veggie dippers of all sorts. Our friend Mary has discovered that it's also the perfect accompaniment for popcorn, her favorite food.

>   **1 tablespoon minced garlic**
>   **¼ cup finely chopped green onion (white and green parts)**
>   **¼ cup olive oil**
>   **2 cups mayonnaise**

Mix garlic, onion, and oil thoroughly. Add mayonnaise and blend mixture well, until oil is absorbed into mayonnaise. Cover and chill.

Makes about 2½ cups

Suggested dippers: *asparagus, red bell pepper, broccoli, potato skins, roast beef, turkey*

Randy Red Salsa

The addition of lime juice to this lively mixture cools it off a bit and also lends a hint of seviche to the taste. It's terrific on its own and also goes well with Kevin's Black Bean dip (see Index), Tom's Splendiferous Guacamole (see Index), and most other Mexican dishes.

2 cups diced fresh tomatoes
¼ cup coarsely chopped onion
1½ teaspoons minced garlic
1 tablespoon coarsely chopped jalapeño pepper
⅛ teaspoon salt
¼ teaspoon dried oregano
1 tablespoon chopped fresh cilantro
¾ teaspoon lime juice

Mix tomatoes and onion well. Add all other ingredients and mix thoroughly. Let stand 1 hour before serving for flavors to meld. May be served at room temperature or chilled.

Makes about 2¼ cups

Suggested dippers: *potato skins, thick green bell pepper wedges, oysters, mushroom caps*

Green Chili Salsa

Green tomatoes and lime juice provide the eye-catching hue, while ja-lapeños and cilantro capture the attention of the taste buds. Not for the faint of heart or palate.

**12 tomatillos (Spanish green tomatoes), husks and
  stems removed**
½ cup chopped yellow onion
5 jalapeño peppers, split, seeds removed
3 tablespoons minced fresh cilantro
1½ teaspoons minced garlic
2 tablespoons lime juice
2 tablespoons olive oil
1½ teaspoons chopped fresh tarragon *or*
  ½ teaspoon dried
½ teaspoon sugar
½ teaspoon salt
⅛ teaspoon black pepper

Coarsely chop tomatillos and place in a bowl. Add all other ingredients and mix well. May be served at room temperature or chilled.

Makes about 3½ cups

Suggested dippers: *corn tortillas, potato skins, celery, jicama, Monterey Jack or cheddar cheese*

59

7
A Crock of Cheese
CHEESE DIPS

SHERRIED CHEDDAR CHEESE

HUNGARIAN SPICED CHEESE

TANGY BLUE CHEESE

GARLIC, CHEESE, AND NUT

BRANDIED GORGONZOLA

HICKORY-SMOKED CHEESE

BARBARA'S BUBBA'S COTTAGE CHEESE

SMOOTH AND SPICY "BOURSIN" CHEESE

Sherried Cheddar Cheese

A comforting, stick-to-your-innards blend, with just enough bite to keep you on your toes! Its flavor reminds us a bit of the homemade cheese concoctions that once graced the bar of many a neighborhood pub.

> **1½ cups shredded sharp cheddar cheese**
> **1 tablespoon sherry**
> **½ cup sour cream**
> **1 tablespoon chopped jalapeño pepper**
> **½ teaspoon hot sauce**
> **¼ teaspoon garlic powder**

Mix cheddar cheese and sherry well. Blend in sour cream. Add all other ingredients. Serve at room temperature.

Makes about 2 cups

Suggested dippers: *celery, carrots, radishes, tomatoes, Polish sausage, cantaloupe, crenshaw, or casaba melon*

Hungarian Spiced Cheese

This dip makes the most of the national spice of Hungary, the mild and slightly sweet variety of paprika. It's inspired by the Hungarian Liptauer cheese spread.

> 1 cup cottage cheese
> 2 teaspoons Hungarian paprika
> 1 teaspoon caraway seeds
> 1 teaspoon mashed capers
> ½ teaspoon dry mustard
> 2 tablespoons chopped green onion (white and green parts)
> ½ cup sour cream

Strain cottage cheese in a colander to remove excess water, then cream in a blender or food processor or with an electric mixer. Put into a bowl and add paprika, caraway seeds, capers, mustard, and green onion. Mix all ingredients together well. Blend in sour cream. Cover and chill.

Makes about 1¾ cups

Suggested dippers: *chicken, string beans, cherry tomatoes, chili peppers*

Tangy Blue Cheese

The dominant taste of blue cheese holds up well to the addition of herbs and spices. It produces a mixture pleasing to blue cheese lovers, who will delight in the chunks floating through this dip, as well as to those with a taste for the tangy.

　　½ **cup blue cheese, crumbled**
　　1½ **cups sour cream**
　　1 **teaspoon minced garlic**
　　2 **tablespoons finely chopped fresh chives** *or* **2**
　　　　teaspoons dried
　　⅛ **teaspoon hot sauce**

Mix blue cheese and sour cream thoroughly. Add other ingredients and blend well. Cover and chill.

Makes about 2 cups

Suggested dippers: *carrots, cherry tomatoes, pineapple, apple, pearapple, cocktail black bread, Italian or French bread chunks*

Garlic, Cheese, and Nut

Rather like a tasty cheese log reincarnated as a dip, this specialty has something for everyone—the cheese lover, the nut lover, and the herb and spice lover.

>   **2 cloves garlic**
>   **½ cup cream cheese, softened**
>   **½ cup sour cream**
>   **¼ cup diced white onion**
>   **1½ teaspoons paprika**
>   **1½ teaspoons curry powder**
>   **1½ teaspoons chili powder**
>   **1 tablespoon chopped fresh dill *or* 1 teaspoon dried**
>   **1 cup shredded sharp cheddar cheese**
>   **⅓ cup chopped walnuts**

Crush garlic with a garlic press and beat into cream cheese until mixture is smooth. Blend in sour cream. Mix in onion, paprika, curry powder, chili powder, and dill. Fold in cheddar cheese and nuts. May be served at room temperature or chilled.

Makes about 2½ cups

Suggested dippers: *sesame crackers, celery, radishes, string beans*

Brandied Gorgonzola

The Italian cousin to the French and Danish blue-veined cheeses, Gorgonzola has a pleasingly sharp taste. The addition of a touch of brandy enriches the dip without hiding the wonderful character of the cheese.

$\frac{1}{2}$ **cup Gorgonzola cheese, softened**
$\frac{3}{4}$ **cup sour cream**
$\frac{1}{4}$ **teaspoon white pepper**
$\frac{3}{4}$ **teaspoon brandy**

Mix Gorgonzola cheese and sour cream until smooth. Add remaining ingredients and blend well. Cover and chill.

Makes about 1¼ cups

Suggested dippers: *cherry tomatoes, green zucchini, jicama, pearapple, anjou pear, nectarine*

Hickory-Smoked Cheese

We like this novel application of hickory-smoked salt, more commonly used to season steaks. Readily available in your supermarket spice section, it imbues this simple mixture with a pleasant, woody aroma.

> 1 cup cottage cheese
> ½ cup sour cream
> 1 tablespoon minced green onion (white and green parts)
> ¼ teaspoon minced garlic
> ½ teaspoon hickory-smoked salt

Blend cottage cheese and sour cream. Add remaining ingredients and mix thoroughly. Cover and chill.

Makes about 1½ cups

Suggested dippers: *potato chips, water crackers, ham, mushrooms, snow peas*

Barbara's Bubba's Cottage Cheese

This is the way our mentor Barbara's grandmother in Massachusetts used to fix up cottage cheese. We like it a lot and think it makes a perfect dip.

¼ **cup diced cucumber**
¼ **cup diced green onion (white and green parts)**
¼ **cup diced radish**
½ **cup cottage cheese**
½ **cup sour cream**
½ **teaspoon celery salt**
¼ **teaspoon black pepper**

Mix cucumber, green onion, and radish. Blend in cottage cheese and sour cream. Add celery salt and pepper, mixing all together thoroughly. Cover and chill.

Makes about 1¾ cups

Suggested dippers: *pita bread triangles, potato skins, seafood, turnips, bok choy*

Smooth and Spicy "Boursin" Cheese

Just like the fine, herbed Boursin cheese found in gourmet shops, this quick and easy homemade version is rich and creamy. We've added walnuts for a bit of a crunch.

½ cup butter, softened
1 cup cream cheese, softened
1 clove garlic, crushed in garlic press
2 teaspoons very finely minced white onion
1 teaspoon Italian seasoning
2 tablespoons milk
2 tablespoons minced walnuts

Cream butter and cream cheese together by hand, then blend garlic into mixture. Add onion and Italian seasoning, mixing well. Blend in milk. Mix in walnuts thoroughly. Serve at room temperature.

Makes about 1¾ cups

Suggested dippers: *apple, lavasch crackers, potato chips, broccoli, cocktail rye bread, dried fruit*

8
A Pot of Beans
BEAN DIPS

KEVIN'S BLACK BEAN

GARLICKY GARBANZO BEAN

DOMESTICATED CHICK-PEA

ZIPPY KIDNEY BEAN

RICH AND CREAMY REFRIED BEAN

LONGHORN QUICK CHILI

CHUNKY KIDNEY BEAN

Kevin's Black Bean

Dedicated to that legion of folks out there who, like Kevin, can't go for too long without a black-bean fix. We like to serve this dish with Randy Red Salsa (see Index).

1½ cups cooked black beans
⅓ cup minced carrot
⅓ cup minced celery
1 tablespoon minced garlic
1 teaspoon dried oregano
1 teaspoon ground cumin
½ teaspoon ground coriander
¼ teaspoon salt
½ cup sour cream
1 tablespoon chopped fresh cilantro leaves *or* 1
   teaspoon dried
Additional cilantro or chopped parsley for garnish

Coarsely mash half the beans by hand. Add remaining whole beans and all other ingredients, mixing well. Cover and chill. Garnish with cilantro or parsley.

Makes about 2¾ cups

Suggested dippers: *bok choy, tortilla chips, corn bread croutons*

Garlicky Garbanzo Bean

Known as hummus, this Middle Eastern treat is quickly becoming an American favorite. Our version has a strong garlic-lemon flavor.

3 cups cooked garbanzo beans (also called chick-peas)
¼ cup water
½ cup tahini (sesame paste)
⅓ cup lemon juice
1½ tablespoons chopped garlic
1 tablespoon salt
1 teaspoon ground cumin
2 tablespoons olive oil
Paprika, lemon slices, and chopped parsley for garnish

Puree beans with water in a food processor or blender to the consistency of a smooth, mashed-potatolike paste. (The beans can also be mashed with water by hand.) Add the tahini, lemon juice, garlic, salt, and cumin. Continue mixing until light and fluffy. Put into a serving bowl and swirl in the olive oil. Sprinkle on paprika and garnish with lemon slices and parsley. Serve at room temperature.

Makes about 4¼ cups

Suggested dippers: *pita bread triangles, celery, carrots, fennel, cheddar cheese*

Domesticated Chick-Pea

A variation on the classic Middle Eastern hummus. In this recipe we've omitted the tahini, resulting in a dip equally as good as, but less dense than, the original.

6 cloves garlic
¼ teaspoon black pepper
1 cup olive oil
½ cup lemon juice
1 tablespoon salt
3 cups cooked chick-peas (also called garbanzo beans)
Chopped parsley for garnish

Place garlic, pepper, olive oil, lemon juice, and salt in a food processor or blender and puree until garlic is finely chopped (if preparing by hand, finely dice and mash garlic, then mix well with other ingredients). Add chick-peas and continue mixing to a smooth paste. Garnish with parsley. May be served at room temperature or chilled.

Makes about 4½ cups

Suggested dippers: *pita bread or toast triangles, scallions, bland water crackers, red cabbage*

Zippy Kidney Bean

This dip's cool yogurt base provides just the right foil for its peppers, chili powder, and hot sauce.

1½ cups cooked red kidney beans
2 teaspoons chopped jalapeño pepper
½ cup shredded sharp cheddar cheese
¼ teaspoon chili powder
¾ cup plain yogurt
½ teaspoon onion powder
¼ teaspoon garlic powder
½ teaspoon hot sauce

In a blender or food processor, puree beans to a coarse paste (beans may also be mashed by hand). Put into a bowl and add all other ingredients. Mix well. Serve at room temperature.

Makes about 2¾ cups

Suggested dippers: *sirloin steak, celery, jicama, cabbage, Swiss cheese*

Rich and Creamy Refried Bean

We recommend using prepared refried beans, available canned in the Mexican food section of most supermarkets.

1 cup refried beans
½ cup sour cream
2 tablespoons chopped black olives
¼ cup chopped fresh tomato
1 teaspoon salsa verde (bottled hot green salsa)
⅛ teaspoon salt
Black pepper to taste
Shredded sharp cheddar cheese for garnish

Mix beans and sour cream thoroughly. Blend in all other ingredients well. Cover and chill. Garnish with cheddar cheese.

Makes about 1¾ cups

Suggested dippers: *cucumber, cheese crackers, jicama, broccoli*

Longhorn Quick Chili

This moderately spicy, but eminently satisfying, southwestern delight can be made in less than 5 minutes and stores well. In fact, the longer it sits in your refrigerator, the better it tastes!

> 1 cup cottage cheese
> 1 15-ounce can chili with beans
> 1 tablespoon hot sauce
> 1 tablespoon lemon juice
> 1½ teaspoons ground cumin
> ¾ cup shredded sharp cheddar cheese

Cream cottage cheese in a blender or food processor or with an electric mixer. Blend in chili well. Add hot sauce, lemon juice, and cumin. Pour into a bowl and mix in cheddar cheese, reserving a little to garnish top. Cover and chill.

Makes about 3¾ cups

Suggested dippers: *tortilla chips, celery, cucumber, bread sticks, deli meat, pickled baby corn, carrots*

Chunky Kidney Bean

Unlike most of our bean dips, this recipe is not aided by a food processor. We prefer mashing the kidney beans here by hand for a coarser texture.

1½ cups cooked kidney beans
¼ cup sour cream
1 teaspoon lemon juice
1 tablespoon ground cumin
1 teaspoon hot sauce
1 tablespoon ground coriander

Mash beans by hand using a fork or the back of a wooden spoon. Blend in sour cream. Add all other ingredients and mix well. Cover and chill.

Makes about 1¾ cups

Suggested dippers: *Polish sausage, celery, corn crackers*

9
The Chafing Dish
HEATED DIPS

BARRY'S ARTICHOKE

UNSTUFFED MUSHROOM

ZESTY ITALIAN ZUCCHINI

STEAMY SMOKED OYSTER

SIAM CHILI DIPPING SAUCE

MEXICAN PINTO BEAN

SWISS CHALET

Barry's Artichoke

Most folks get their artichoke hearts canned, as our recipe calls for. Barry is perhaps the only one around who would relish the challenge of downing enough fresh artichoke leaves to supply the requisite amount of hearts.

1 14-ounce can artichoke hearts (not marinated)
¼ cup grated Parmesan cheese
¼ cup grated Romano cheese
1 cup shredded mozzarella cheese
1 small garlic clove, minced fine
½ cup mayonnaise
Paprika for garnish

Rinse and drain artichoke hearts, then remove and discard fuzzy chokes. Chop artichoke hearts. Mix all ingredients well and place in greased 1½-quart casserole. Dust top of mixture lightly with paprika. Bake at 325° F for 25 minutes. Serve hot.

Makes about 3 cups

Suggested dippers: *French or Italian bread, water crackers, snow peas, carrots, salami slices, seafood chunks*

Unstuffed Mushroom

If you like stuffed mushrooms, you'll love this dip. We take the usual ingredients for stuffed mushrooms and, instead of putting them in the mushrooms, put them with the mushrooms, in the dip.

1 pound whole white button mushrooms, diced
1 cup shredded Monterey Jack cheese
**¼ cup finely crumbled bacon (3-4 slices cooked) *or*
    imitation bacon bits**
½ cup sour cream
1 teaspoon Worcestershire sauce
4 drops hot sauce
Seasoned bread crumbs for garnish

Combine mushrooms, Monterey Jack cheese, and bacon. Stir in sour cream. Blend in Worcestershire sauce and hot sauce. Place mixture in a 1-quart casserole and top with bread crumbs. Bake at 350° F for 15 minutes, or until cheese has melted. Serve hot.

Makes about 2½ cups

Suggested dippers: *tomatoes, bell peppers, chili peppers, bread sticks*

Zesty Italian Zucchini

A loaf of bread (Italian, of course), a jug of wine (Soave, perhaps), and thou are all that are needed to transform this dip into a cozy supper.

3 cups shredded zucchini
1 cup cream cheese, softened
2 tablespoons milk
2 eggs
¼ cup grated Romano cheese
¼ cup grated Parmesan cheese
½ cup finely chopped yellow onion
2 tablespoons minced fresh parsley *or* 2 teaspoons
** dried**
½ teaspoon salt
½ teaspoon dried oregano

Place shredded zucchini in a colander, squeeze out any excess water, and set aside. Beat cream cheese to a smooth consistency. Blend in milk and eggs. Mix in all other ingredients, including zucchini, and place in a greased 1½-quart casserole. Bake at 350° F for 20 minutes, or until heated through and bubbly. Serve hot.

Makes about 5 cups

Suggested dippers: *Italian bread chunks, bell peppers, hot dogs, Genoa sausage*

82

Steamy Smoked Oyster

The oyster has long had a somewhat shady reputation and remains shrouded in mystery about its supposed power as an aphrodisiac. We can say one thing for sure—these oysters will entice you to fall in love with this hot dip!

1 tablespoon butter
½ cup sliced almonds
1 cup cream cheese, softened
1 tablespoon milk
Black pepper to taste
1½ teaspoons prepared horseradish
2 tablespoons chopped white onion
2 3.6-ounce cans smoked oysters, rinsed, drained, and
    mashed with fork

Melt butter in a frying pan. Brown almonds on all sides in the melted butter and set aside. Beat cream cheese until smooth and blend in milk. Add pepper, horseradish, and chopped onion, blending well. Fold in oysters. Pour into a casserole dish. Sprinkle browned almonds on top. Bake at 375° F for 20 to 30 minutes, or until bubbly. Serve hot.

Makes about 2¼ cups

Suggested dippers: *potato chips, tortilla chips, cheese crackers, bell peppers, fennel, zucchini*

Siam Chili Dipping Sauce

A slightly sweeter variation of the classic spicy dipping sauce from Thailand, both exotic and easily prepared. The chili paste with garlic is readily available in the Oriental food section of most supermarkets.

⅓ **cup water**
⅓ **cup white vinegar**
⅓ **cup granulated sugar**
½ **teaspoon chili paste with garlic**
¼ **teaspoon salt**
½ **teaspoon minced garlic**

In a heavy saucepan (preferably enamel), bring water to a boil. Add remaining ingredients. Return to a boil, then cook 2 to 3 minutes, until sugar has dissolved. Serve hot.

Makes about 1 cup

Suggested dippers: *fried wonton, egg rolls, noodle chips, seafood*

Mexican Pinto Bean

Smooth and bubbly, but with a bite, this dip is sure to transport you south of the border faster than a Tijuana taxi! To keep its meter ticking, serve in a chafing dish or fondue pot over a low flame.

3 cups cooked pinto beans
¼ cup water
½ cup shredded Monterey Jack cheese
½ teaspoon chili powder
1½ teaspoons salsa verde (bottled hot green salsa)

Puree beans to a coarse paste in a blender or food processor or mash by hand. Place bean paste in a saucepan with the water and heat. Mix in all other ingredients and simmer until cheese is melted, about 5 minutes. Serve hot.

Makes about 3¾ cups

Suggested dippers: *tortilla chips, black cocktail rye bread, bell peppers, celery, Monterey Jack cheese*

Swiss Chalet

You'll think you're by the fireside in an Alpine ski lodge when you dip into this hot ham-and-Swiss mixture.

> **1 cup dry white wine**
> **2 cups shredded Swiss cheese**
> **1 tablespoon flour**
> **1 tablespoon brandy**
> **1 clove garlic, crushed in a garlic press**
> **1 tablespoon finely diced white onion**
> **Black pepper to taste**
> **¼ cup finely diced smoked ham**
> **Nutmeg to garnish**

Put wine in a saucepan over medium-high heat. Mix together Swiss cheese and flour and add gradually to wine, stirring constantly, until all cheese is melted and mixture is smooth. Take off heat and add brandy, garlic, onion, pepper, and ham. Dust top with nutmeg. Serve hot.

Makes about 3¼ cups

Suggested dippers: *apple, artichoke hearts, crackers, French bread chunks, ham, salami*

10

Seren*dip-it*ies

OUR ALL-TIME FAVORITE DIPS

FAR EAST PEANUT DIPPING SAUCE

BAVARIAN LIVERWURST

DOWN AND DIRTY APPLE CHUTNEY

LARRY'S SPICY PEANUT YOGURT

Far East Peanut Dipping Sauce

We think this blend of thick, rich peanut butter, spicy chili and garlic, and lingering sesame is a special treat.

> **1 tablespoon soy sauce**
> **4 teaspoons water**
> **2 teaspoons rice wine vinegar**
> **1 cup chunky peanut butter**
> **1 tablespoon sesame oil**
> **1 teaspoon chili paste with garlic**
> **⅛ teaspoon cayenne pepper**
> **¼ cup mayonnaise**

Mix soy sauce, water, and vinegar and set aside. Put peanut butter in a bowl and mix in sesame oil thoroughly. Then mix in chili paste and cayenne pepper. Add soy sauce mixture and mix well. Blend in mayonnaise. Serve at room temperature.

Makes about 1¼ cups

Suggested dippers: *beef satay, shrimp, crayfish, sesame crackers, scallions, cherry tomatoes, snow peas*

Bavarian Liverwurst

Hearty liverwurst is combined with sour cream and other goodies to produce a rich, but surprisingly delicate and elegant, dip.

1 cup liverwurst
½ cup sour cream
¼ cup minced white onion
1 tablespoon dill pickle relish
1 tablespoon Dijon mustard
½ teaspoon white pepper

Blend liverwurst and sour cream until smooth and creamy. Add all other ingredients and mix well. May be served at room temperature or chilled.

Makes about 1¾ cups

Suggested dippers: *cucumber, cherry tomatoes, radishes, asparagus, cocktail rye bread, lavasch crackers*

Down and Dirty Apple Chutney

This concoction, which we discovered quite by accident, is probably the quickest and easiest chutney recipe around—and it's quite good!

1 cup natural, unsweetened chunky applesauce
¼ cup honey
¼ cup raisins
4 teaspoons lemon juice
1 tablespoon tarragon vinegar
2 tablespoons dark brown sugar
½ teaspoon curry powder
1 teaspoon celery salt

Mix applesauce and honey. Add raisins and mix well. Blend in lemon juice and vinegar. Add other ingredients and mix well. Cover and chill.

Makes about 1¾ cups

Suggested dippers: *pound cake cubes, dried fruit, steak, apricots, melon, Italian bread chunks, croutons*

Larry's Spicy Peanut Yogurt

This dip is dedicated to our friend Larry, who argues, rather persuasively at times, that peanut butter is the primary nutrient and cornerstone of Western civilization. In our search for the ideal peanut butter dip, we found that peanut butter blends surprisingly well with yogurt, which thins it out and adds a tangy flavor.

$\frac{1}{4}$ **cup peanut butter**
1 cup plain yogurt
1 teaspoon ground coriander
$\frac{1}{2}$ **teaspoon cayenne pepper**
$\frac{1}{8}$ **teaspoon salt**

Blend peanut butter and yogurt well. Add other ingredients and mix thoroughly. Cover and chill.

Makes about 1¼ cups

Suggested dippers: *seafood, kiwi, plums, saltines*

11

The Dessert Board
SWEET DIPS

SILKY APRICOT CHEESE

ORANGE-GINGER

GOLDEN CITRUS-RAISIN

CHOCOLATE CHIP CHEESECAKE

ANITA'S EASY CHOCOLATE DIPPING SAUCE

MIDGET'S MANGO CREAM

PINEAPPLE-WALNUT

DOROTHY'S BANANA BREAD

STRAWBERRY GRAND MARNIER CHEESECAKE

Silky Apricot Cheese

We think this is one of the creamiest dessert dips ever to grace a graham cracker or a windmill cookie. You can vary its texture by the type of preserves used, which range in consistency from spreadlike to chunky with fruit.

¾ cup apricot preserves
2 teaspoons brandy
1 cup cream cheese, softened
1 cup sour cream
1 teaspoon almond extract
¼ cup blanched, slivered almonds

In a small bowl, mix together apricot preserves and brandy. Set aside. Beat cream cheese to a creamy consistency. Blend in sour cream and almond extract until smooth. Add apricot preserves–brandy mixture and blend well. Fold in almonds. Cover and chill.

Makes about 3 cups

Suggested dippers: *vanilla wafers, pound cake cubes, Muenster or Monterey Jack cheese, chocolate chunks*

Orange-Ginger

We thought of this dip while eating a favorite Chinese dish that contains both oranges and ginger. While the effect achieved by combining the flavors in a base of sour cream and cream cheese is totally different, they blend equally well here—producing a refreshing mixture in which the citrus provides a nice balance to the aggressive taste of ginger.

1½ teaspoons dried ginger
½ cup cream cheese, softened
½ cup sour cream
¼ cup orange juice
½ teaspoon orange zest

Beat ginger and cream cheese to a smooth consistency. Blend in sour cream. Add orange juice and orange zest and mix well. Cover and chill.

Makes about 1¼ cups

Suggested dippers: *apricots, chicken, pound cake cubes*

Golden Citrus-Raisin

We prefer to use golden raisins for purely aesthetic reasons—they look terrific mixed in with the orange and pecans. But any raisins will work.

1 orange, seeded and quartered with rind on
1 cup chopped pecans
2 cups golden raisins
½ cup mayonnaise
½ cup plain yogurt

Combine all ingredients in a food processor or blender and process to a chunky consistency. Cover and chill.

Makes about 4½ cups

Suggested dippers: *ladyfingers, plum wafers, pineapple, ham, chicken drumettes, celery*

Chocolate Chip Cheesecake

The idea for this recipe comes from a certain mild-mannered editor for a major metropolitan publishing house. All that's missing for a perfect cheese-cake filling are the eggs, but our editor likes it better this way. As long as it's not a real cheesecake, it's fair game for late-night snacking, even in the midst of a diet.

> ½ cup raisins
> 1 tablespoon brandy
> 2 cups cream cheese, softened
> ½ cup whipping cream
> ½ teaspoon vanilla extract
> ¼ cup dark brown sugar
> 1 teaspoon cinnamon
> ½ cup mini chocolate chips
> Additional cinnamon for garnish

Mix raisins and brandy (making sure all raisins are coated) and let soak for 15 minutes. In a separate bowl, beat cream cheese and whipping cream until well blended and smooth. Add vanilla. Blend in brown sugar and cinnamon. Mix in "slushed" raisins and chocolate chips. Garnish with a light dusting of cinnamon. Serve at room temperature.

Makes about 3¾ cups

Suggested dippers: *graham crackers, honeydew melon, strawberries, peaches, dried fruit, pound cake cubes*

Anita's Easy Chocolate Dipping Sauce

Easy to prepare—and easy to devour! Inspired by Anita, a culinary student who helps out in our store and who always seems to be dipping chocolate. Anita suggested a simple recipe, and we made it even simpler.

> **8 ounces milk chocolate**
> **½ cup whipping cream**
> **1–2 tablespoons hazelnut-flavored liqueur**

Melt chocolate in a double boiler. Allow to cool until tepid, then blend in whipping cream and liqueur. Serve immediately.

Makes about 1½ cups

Suggested dippers: *fresh or dried fruit, vanilla wafers, ladyfingers, pound cake cubes, plain cookies, pretzels*

Midget's Mango Cream

Like our diminutive friend Kathy, who is nicknamed "the Midget," this recipe is compact and classy—proving that less is indeed often more.

1 cup cream cheese, softened
½ cup mango chutney

Beat cream cheese to a smooth and creamy consistency. Mix in mango chutney well. Cover and chill.

Makes about 1½ cups

Suggested dippers: *sesame crackers, pineapple, melon, crab, chicken, ham*

Pineapple-Walnut

If you think this sounds a little like one of your mother's jazzed-up gelatin molds, you're right. But don't hold that against the ingredients, which have found a more meaningful existence reincarnated as a dip.

1 cup cottage cheese
½ cup sour cream
1 cup crushed pineapple
¼ cup chopped walnuts
½ teaspoon lemon juice
¼ teaspoon lemon zest

Cream cottage cheese in a blender or food processor or with an electric mixer. Blend in sour cream. Add all other ingredients and mix well. Cover and chill.

Makes about 2¾ cups

Suggested dippers: *vanilla wafers, chicken, pear, strawberries*

Dorothy's Banana Bread

The inspiration for this dip was Dorothy, our friend Barbara's daughter, who has a fiendish habit of gobbling up the banana bread batter before it ever gets to the oven. The addition of oatmeal provides added texture without intruding on the "nana" taste.

> 1 cup mashed, very ripe bananas (2-3 bananas)
> 1 teaspoon lemon juice
> 1 teaspoon vanilla extract
> ¼ teaspoon salt
> ½ cup sugar
> 1½ teaspoons cinnamon
> ¼ teaspoon ground nutmeg
> ½ cup raw "quick" oatmeal (1-minute, quick-cooking
>   oatmeal, not the individual-serving "instant"
>   oatmeal)

Mix banana and lemon juice well. Blend in other ingredients. Serve immediately.

Makes about 2 cups

Suggested dippers: *fresh or dried fruit, chocolate wafers, pound cake cubes, vanilla wafers*

Strawberry Grand Marnier Cheesecake

Our favorite way to have our Grand Marnier and eat it too, as it were. We prefer to use fresh strawberries, because they're crunchier and more flavorful, but frozen will do in a pinch.

$\frac{1}{2}$ **cup crushed strawberries**
$\frac{1}{4}$ **cup finely chopped walnuts**
$\frac{1}{4}$ **cup dark brown sugar**
$\frac{1}{3}$ **cup Grand Marnier liqueur**
1 cup cream cheese, softened
1 cup sour cream

Reserve 1 tablespoon each of strawberries and walnuts for garnish. In a small bowl, mix together strawberries, brown sugar, and liqueur. Set aside. Blend cream cheese and sour cream until smooth. Add the strawberry mixture and blend well. Fold in walnuts. Mound the reserved strawberries in the center, ringed with the reserved walnuts. Cover and chill.

Makes about 3½ cups

Suggested dippers: *chocolate wafers or crackers, graham crackers, chocolate chunks, ladyfingers, banana*

Index